My Dad Is a GOOD Cop

By: Kacy Chambers

This book is dedicated to ALL of the GOOD cops, the Green, Golden, and Bryson families.

Special dedication to Sydrea Bryson, Candace Green, and Kendal Golden.

My dad is a good dad and a good police officer.

He works a lot of hours to help protect the city.

I miss him when he is at work.

There are a lot of people in the world. Some are good and some are bad.

Some of the good people become cops and some of the bad people become cops too.

GOOD

BAD

I know that my dad is a good cop because he does the right thing and teaches me to do the same.

My dad does not arrest people just to be mean or because of their skin color.

He only arrests the people who do bad things.

When he sees a cop doing WRONG, he lets them know that they are doing WRONG.

He ALWAYS does the RIGHT thing, even if it means that it will make others mad.

RIGHT

WRONG

When people call 911, my dad shows up to help them.

9-1-1

When I grow up, I want to be a good person just like my dad.

Maybe, I will decide to be a GOOD cop too.

More of my books

Visit www.authorkacychambers.com to learn more.

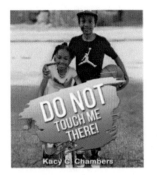

Do Not Touch Me There

Sometimes Grandma and
Grandpa Forget

Do Not Touch Me There Safe
Place Journal for Young Girls

Do Not Touch Me There Safe
Place Journal for Young Boys

Made in the USA
Columbia, SC
06 April 2022